# DIVINATIONBYPLAYINGCARDS

*an updated approach to cartomancy*

DEDICATED TO THE MEMORY OF PRIEST
OSWAN CHAMANI

Spirit of Life Center for Positive Changes
Columbia, Maryland

To order additional copies of this book, contact:
Xlibris
844-714-8691
www.Xlibris.com
Orders@Xlibris.com

Book Designer: Michael E. Anthony

ISBN:    Softcover        978-1-4134-0542-2

Print information available on the last page

Rev. date: 10/09/2020

# DIVINATIONBYPLAYINGCARDS

*an updated approach to cartomancy*

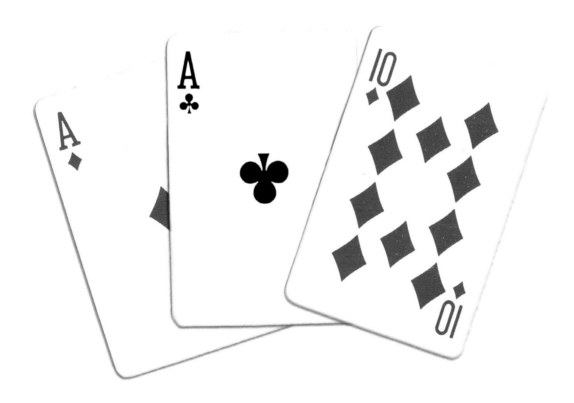

FÁDÙNMÁDÉ

# CONTENTS

# INTRODUCTION

This is not another "how to" book on reading cards - rather it is a study providing ideas to stimulate your imagination. The goal is to unlock the door to insight and understanding.

The origin of the playing cards and their use as a tool of divination are uncertain. Cards have been used for centuries for entertainment and divination. However, if one were to ask where the cards came from the answers would be vague at best. There is much speculation and many unsupported theories about the origin of cards. There are theories involving the origin of cards from Atlantis to ancient Africa and Asia. Cards have been studied, discussed and their symbols dissected by researchers/scholars and all of their work has not led to a particular source of the cards. Still today there are people who are trying to discern the origin of the cards. However, the exact origin of the cards and the art of divination remain hidden.

It is widely believed that the ordinary pack of playing cards is derived from the Tarot. Like the Tarot cards, the playing cards carry a combination of symbols, shapes and colors which can stimulate the subconscious to bring forth insights from ancient wisdom, past events and insights on today's possibilities. They represent deep and profound psychological and spiritual truths.

The ordinary pack of playing cards is related to the minor arcana of the Tarot. Just as in the Tarot, the playing cards have associations with the elements through their suits. There are also associations to numerology and astrology.

Even with the long history of use, cards have been the center of controversy at times. Cards were banned by certain royal courts in the fourteenth century and banned by the church, too, in the fifteenth century. Yet cards are still popular today and can still be found in many homes used for the same purposes - entertainment and divination.

In addition to being used for entertainment and divination, cards have seen unusual uses. For example, it is known that in 1765 playing cards were used as admission tickets to classes at the University of Pennsylvania. This follows reason since Benjamin Franklin was a leading manufacturer of playing cards, first in Boston, and later in Philadelphia.

Cards have played many roles through out history and we do know that the cards and stories of their power of divination go back at least several hundred years. The cards when used as a tool of divination, are thought provoking. When used properly and with respect, the cards will reveal to you some future aspects of your life that are not apparent to you at the present. Divination by cards is an ancient practice and it is still popular world wide. In addition, divination by cards is as valid today as it ever was and fun to learn.

# W H A T T H E S U I T S M E A N

There are four suits in the standard pack of playing cards: hearts, clubs, diamonds and spades.

These suits have many  attributes, they represent the four ways in which we perceive any thing: through  intuition- clubs, through emotions- hearts, through thoughts- spades and through the physical senses (sensation)- diamonds.

On another level we attribute clubs (intuition) to the superconscious mind; hearts (emotions) to the subconscious; spades (thoughts) to the conscious mind and diamonds (sensations) to the physical. This symbolizes the mental, emotional, spiritual and physical nature of humans.

The suits correspond to the essentials of our existence on earth. There is a correspondence to the four seasons of the year, the four directions and the four elements. Clubs are associated with summer; hearts with autumn, diamonds with winter and spades with spring. The four directions: clubs represent the south, hearts the west, diamonds the north and spades the east. The four elements are clubs for fire; hearts for water; diamonds for earth  and spades for air.

In the middle ages the suits represented a level or class of society: spades represented nobility;  hearts represented the clergy; diamonds the merchants and clubs were the symbol for the working class. In divination, the suit of hearts symbolizes love, and generally hearts are a good sign in a spread.  Hearts are associated with any emotional aspect of one's life and  relationships whether business or personal. Hearts are associated with the element of water. Individuals  represented by hearts are usually people oriented and will see their relationships (family, personal or business) as very important.

Clubs correspond to progress, growth, and creativity. Communication, intuition, thinking and some financial situations are expressed in this suit. When clubs are dominant in a suit, expect a quick demonstration of your desire. Clubs are associated with the element of fire. People identifying with clubs are thinkers, good communicators and are often intuitive.

The diamonds are business oriented. In general terms they represent possessions, financial matters and jobs. When diamonds are the dominant suit in a spread expect pleasant conditions to be in the process of taking form or happening. Diamonds represent the earth element. Those who are diamonds are practical, but will sometimes have a desire for status and a materialistic outlook.

Spades show that change is in progress. When spades dominate a spread there is tremendous activity going on in one's life. When endings are indicated there is always a new beginning. Spades are connected to mental activity and the element of air. People represented by spades are decisive, professional people.

# THE NUMBERS COUNT

An important part of the reading is to take into consideration the numbers on the cards that are revealed in the reading. Included here are broad guides for the indication of the numbers from one to ten.

## ACE

Beginnings          Potentials

Births              Roots

Openings            Totality

## TWO

Balance             Duality

Choices             Harmony

Cooperation         Union

## THREE

Creation            Insecurity

Expression          Productivity

Indecision          Resolution

## FOUR

Boundaries          Order

Centering           Peace

Foundation          Stability

## FIVE

Changes             Multiple choices

Freedom             Travel

Movement            Uncertainty

## SIX

Assistance          Mediation

Destiny             Stability

Karma               Service

## SEVEN

Challenges          Beginnings

Directions          Spirituality

Insights            Tests

## EIGHT

Compassion          Power

Energy              Satisfaction

Order               Success

## NINE

Completions/Endings     Forgiveness

Disappointment          Healing

Fate                    Tolerance

## TEN

Completion          New beginning

Good news           Perfection

Happiness           Transformation

# WHAT THE CARDS MEAN

Each card is usually associated with some aspect of daily life in a reading, so for simplicity, these aspects will be referred to as the meaning of the cards. Some meanings are universal, but by no means absolute. These attributes are fine for memorizing in order to identify a particular card. However, as you get more in tune to the meanings of the cards, your definitions will probably differ from the ones you memorized in your early training. This is not unusual since every one has a different set of life experiences. When you give new or different attributes to the cards that indicates that the subconscious has received the symbols and is guiding you to a more in depth reading.

Aces introduce these aspects: beginnings, births, newness, opportunities, openings, potential, desire and the basic message of the suit which it represents.

Ace ♥

Emotional fulfillment

Good news

Intuition

Joy

New love

Pleasure

The home

Triumph over adversity

Ace ♦

Contract

Good fortune

Material fulfillment/monetary gains

New business venture

New goals

Practicality

Prosperity

Security

Success

Ace ♣

Creativity

Excitement

Good luck

New business or social venture

New ideas

New outlook

New plans

Spiritual beginning

Ace ♠

New concepts and ideas

New job (also a desire for work)

Power card

The mind card (clarity of mind)

Transformation

Truth

Doubts / worries

Secrets

Twos focus on balance, harmony, choices, indecision, duality and union.

## Two ♥

A strong love
Birth
Friendship
Happy events
Reconciliation
Romance
Union
Wedding

## Two ♣

A change of circumstances
A time card (with the 2 ♠, time is running out)
Discussions
Large plans
Partnership
Something coming in pairs
Studying

## Two ♦

A check (may be a refund)
Bids for contracts/ business deals
Business negotiations
Gains
Material choices
Messages about money/finances
Money

## Two ♠

Arbitrations
Cooperation also compromise
Decisions
Major change
Partings
Secrets
Suppressed anger
Suspension

Threes express creativity, productivity, indecision, insecurity, synthesis, resolution, and expression.

## Three ♥

A mystical interest
A positive outcome
A triangle (in a relationship reading)
A trip
Celebration
Minor wish card
Renewal

## Three ♦

Contracts
Generating money
Job
Legal matters
Maybe two sources of earning money
Money from one's creativity
Success (refers to work or job)
Money worries

## Three ♣

Creativity
Good luck (the clover leaf)
Growth in business
Money coming from something in the past
Power or strength for a major achievement
Start of a profitable business/employment
Writer's card

## Three ♠

End of emotional problems
Fast arrival of good news
Incompatibility
Pain (emotional)
Stress
Trouble from the outside
Uncertainty

Fours represent a foundation, boundary, good supply, completion, as well as peace, contentment, stability and order.

## Four ♥

A marriage and family card
A merger or partnership
A need to accept love and to love one's self
Emotional blessings
Boredom
Discontent
Unfulfilled in romance

## Four ♦

Business deals
Establishing roots
Financial security
Material security
Money satisfaction
Power
Resources

## Four ♣

Achievement
Blessings
Celebrations
Mental peace
Thanksgiving
Tranquility
Fixed attitudes

## Four ♠

A new beginning after something has ended
Graduation/certification
Meditation
Mental foundation
A need to rest or retreat
Recovery
Should recognize self (and needs)
Stress / frustration

Fives bring changes, a move, travel, movement, restlessness and uncertainty.

## Five ♥

A relationship unfolding into a more fulfilling phase
Creativity
Change of heart
Disappointment/dissatisfaction
Divorce/separation
Jealousy
Unsettled emotions

## Five ♦

Clearing up important legal
and financial matters
Legal papers
Money changing hands (spending money)
Money subject to change
Possible move
Real estate event
Worry over material things

## Five ♣

All written communications including contracts
Be open to new things, new ideas, new people
Business change
Change of mind or plans
Move of residence
Overcoming obstacles
Restlessness/unable to commit

## Five ♠

Travel
Moving the home
Divorce
Misunderstanding
Personal strife
Separation
Slander

The sixes indicate karma, destiny, stability, mediation, responsibility and  assistance.

## Six ♥

A love from the past
Love debts
Peaceful relationship
Adjustment
Completions
Self  sacrifice
Being too emotional

## Six ♦

A "go ahead" sign in business affairs
A raise or promotion
Increased financial activities
Money stable
Putting out money (repayment)
Signing papers

## Six ♣

Balance
Choice of ways to make money
Goals and progress validated
Pay off time
Revitalization
Rewards
Victory

## Six ♠

A journey
Breaking away
Fate; forces beyond your control
Gains, but with hard work
Leaving a bad space
Progress
Troubles soon over

Sevens deal with challenges and tests, spirituality, insight, release and new directions.

## Seven

A good news card

A new door opening

A nice surprise

Favorable change in environment

Potential for happiness

Several possibilities

Emotional greed

## Seven

Employment opportunities,
improved money conditions

Negotiations

Personal success

Positive business and social changes

Holding beliefs that are limiting

Release negativity

## Seven ♦

A job offer or business opportunity

A lucky break

Career change

Change in income

Great prospects in a new business venture

Successful career negotiations

## Seven ♠

Confidence, hope and faith

New plans

New hopes

Apprehension

Drinking card

Feeling cheated

Need to extend more effort

Eights hold power, energy, organization, success, order and satisfaction.

## Eight ♥

A power card

Happy events

Healing

Journey

Moving away from the old and on to

something more interesting

New beginning

## Eight ♦

Financial power

Money "red tape" cleared

Money to spend

New endeavors with success

Practical developments

Next to 7 ♦ expect a lotto win

Short journeys in connection with

business

## Eight ♣

Conversation/communication

Creative breakthrough

Events happening rapidly

Luck and success

Quick courtship

Successful journey

Letting go of the old

## Eight ♠

Overcoming obstacles

Potential  and opportunity

Isolation

Loneliness

Mental fatigue

Seeing a doctor

Temporary problems

Nines suggest endings or completions, fate, healing, disappointment and success.

## Nine ♥

The WISH card

Attainment

Happiness

Pleasure

Universal love

Letting go of anything that is no longer valid

## Nine ♦

Increase

New business venture

Offers and proposals

Opportunities

Preparing for a new cycle

Promotion

Spending money

## Nine ♣

Achievement

A profitable opportunity

Settling a business deal

Wisdom and discipline

Mental disappointment/emotional tension

Negativity vanishing

Self doubt

## Nine ♠

Difficulties are over; forced into a better
life style by the past

Redirect negative energy in order to get
back on course

Nagging worries

Self cruelty

Tens are endings preparing for new beginnings, transformation, success, happiness, good news and perfection.

## Ten ♥

Big and favorable turning points

Contentment

Family fun

Good news

Joy

New phase of an existing relationship
or a new relationship

Special occasion

## Ten ♦

Completion with a new beginning

A new chapter in life

Prosperity and wealth

A (positive) career card

Financial growth

Change

Highest card for success

## Ten ♣

Changing sites

Fortunate business move

Journey

Overcoming limitations

Preparation for a new venture

Needless worry

Too much on the mind

## Ten ♠

Completion of a major cycle

Current problems ending

Wheel of fortune

A body of water (possibly a trip
across water)

Disappointment

Fear of loss and defeat

Confinement

Jacks generally represent young people and messengers. However, idealism, creativity, new ideas given through meditation and intuition also come with the energy of the Jacks.

## Jack ♥

A lucky card adding strength to nearby cards

An idea which brings good changes

New feelings and attitudes

Pleasure

Spiritual motivation

The lover (or cupid)

Unexpected money

## Jack ♦

Ambitious person

Communication

Financial success

Persistence leading to rewards

Pleasant news

The salesman

## Jack ♣

A business friend or partner

A journey

Change of residence

Good news

New ideas

Opportunity leading to changes

Seeking new direction

## Jack ♠

Creative, intuitive thinking

Good news about business

Quick changes

Spiritual initiate

The "con-artist" type personality

Queens refer to women or mature female images in general, and the four queens have been compared to the four Marys of the Bible. The queens, each with distinct attributes, are generally service oriented.

## Queen ♥

Good luck

Help with the events unfolding in one's life

The marriage and family card

The mother and devoted wife

## Queen ♣

Confidence

Seeing life from a different perspective

Self discovery

Success in business

The spiritual explorer

Wisdom

## Queen ♦

Competent

Materialistic

Practical, hardworking, organized woman

Security and success

Wealth

Well-being

## Queen ♠

An intellectual

Can be a vindictive person

One who does not like interference

One who has experienced sorrow

Triumph

Unusual chance for success

Kings are full of vitality and authority.  A king indicates mastery over the aspect of life represented by the suit.

## King ♥

Excellent diplomat

Perfect companion

The lover

Time to get in touch with your feelings

Trust intuition (listen to inner voice)

## King ♦

Achievement

Established work

Healer

Material gains and attainment

The financial wizard

The producer

## King ♣

A decisive male, makes decisions instantly

Communicator

Evolution and change on a deep level

Long term career

Positive male power

The practical one

## King ♠

The intellect

Professional, Powerful and Authoritative

Highly analytical

Restrictive

Defensive

In many cases, the joker is the forgotten and most misunderstood card in the pack.  Many times the joker is discarded and not used at all.  There are layouts and readings where you might want to include the joker. This card is sometimes referred to as "the wild card."

A few attributes of the joker:

Things not manifest- still unknown- things still in thought form.

The joker often represents taking chances or acting without careful planning.

The joker is an indication of surprise.

# PAIRS

There are many ways to approach a reading. Your own individual approach will develop as you work with the cards. What ever your approach, it is necessary to observe some basics.

As you start a reading it is very important to look at which suit dominates the spread, this will show you immediately what area the person who is seeking the reading needs advice. Sometimes the cards will not speak to the question or the problem which the person wants advice on but will speak to the most important concerns of the person (what s/he really needs to know). This is usually the case when a reading does not seem pertinent to you (the reader) or the person at the time the reading is done.

The next consideration is the meaning of the individual cards. As the cards are read and used with frequency, you will begin to receive new or additional attributes for the cards. Your subconscious has received the symbols and is guiding you to your own interpretations. This is important because now the cards are associating with your intuitive mind and your readings will become more meaningful.

As you become more in tune to the meanings of the card, your meanings will differ more and more from the ones that you memorized in your early training. This is not unusual since every one has a different set of life experiences. When you have taken these things into consideration, there are at least three more important items that should be considered. When the cards fall in pairs in the reading, when there are multiples (three or four cards of the same value) in the spread and the reader should also consider certain combinations of cards. These aspects expand the reading and help to further define situations, conditions and people in the spread.

When ACES are paired,
the possible meanings are:

A change of place

An affair or union

Partnership

Reunion

Surprise

A pair of red aces–a surprise

Ace♠ followed by either red ace–a favorable change

A♦ and the A♣ –relocation/change of place


When TWOS are paired:

Balance

Separation

Things coming in pairs

Union; good friendship

2♣ and 2♦ –an unexpected message


Two hearts–domestic happiness; love is an important part of life.

Two clubs–gradual rise in status; others seeking information


When THREES are paired:

Choice

Promising outlook

Open to options

A good harvest


When FOURS are paired:

Practical, solid situation if the spade is not included

Interest in material things and worldly pleasures

4♦ and 4♣ = Money coming

4♥ and 4♠ = Bad news


When FIVES are paired:

Reach for your goal; what you want is within your grasp

Uncertainty


When SIXES are paired:

Things making a turn for better luck

A beautiful friendship

## When SEVENS are paired:

A change in one's life and luck

Mutual love

Unexpected event; good news

7♥ and 7♦ –Hot romance

7♣ and 7♦ –New career with big pay

## When EIGHTS are paired:

A good time

A passing infatuation

Dreams of love

New experience and knowledge

8♥ and 8♣ –Happiness assured

## When NINES are paired:

A happy surprise involving your wish

Change in residence

Contentment

Gains

Prosperity

9♣ and 9♦ –Business, financial and social life looking up

9♥ and 9♠ –Your wish will come, but there are some obstacles

## When TENS are paired:

A short trip

Change of fortune or career

Change in resident or environment

Extremely good news

Unexpected luck

10♦ and 10♥ –Success and good news;  wedding

The two black tens–A trip near water

The two red tens–Moving forward toward better things

## When JACKS are paired:

Discussions at hand

Legal actions

Someone returns

Malicious schemes

## When QUEENS are paired:

A meeting

Gossip

Secrets betrayed

Q♣ and Q♠ –gossip

## When KINGS are paired:

Advisors

News

Partners

An important meeting is imminent

King♠ and King♣ an active politician

# M U L T I P L E S

Three or four  cards of the same value in a spread.

## ACE

Three aces without the A♠ –New beginnings with good opportunities

Three aces including the A♠ –New beginnings but with a few obstacles

Three aces–Harmony, good news and lucky break

            An opportunity to start anew and have success

Four aces–A big chance or a big change; success, joy and celebration; Business and career issues

          A strong indicator of good luck

Four  aces with the A♠ followed by a red ace–A favorable change

## TWOS

Three twos–Everything happens at once; changes; whatever  comes is doubled; partnerships flourish

Four twos–Crossroads; when something ends, a new phase replaces the old

         Cooperation and teamwork

## THREES

Three of the four threes in the same spread–Stability; success as well as good fortune

          Big change in work and when the 3♦ is included an adjustment;

      3♠ –awareness on a higher plane

Four threes–Hope, happiness and good fortune

## FOURS

Three fours in the same spread–A small gathering

Major money

Four fours–A crowd

## FIVES

Three fives–Giving and caring for others

        Good creative energy

        Satisfaction; difficulties surmounted

        Success and awards

Four fives–A major turning point in life

## SIXES

Three sixes–A family get together

        Crucial decision needs to be made

Hard work, but one's efforts are rewarded

Four sixes–Completing tasks

        Tying up loose ends

        Happiness

## SEVENS

Three sevens–A big change in the three most important areas in one's life; the missing area is determined by attributes of the missing suit

Fulfillment

Major career change or new project

Four sevens–A huge change, other cards in the spread determine the quality and kind of change

## EIGHTS

Three eights–A journey; possibly a change of location

        Less burdens

        Power and recognition

        Taking a trip in hopes of meeting someone

Four eights–A short journey

        A warning to weigh any new proposal carefully

        Worries


## NINES

Three nines–Changes in philosophy and attitude

        Health, wealth and happiness without the 9♠

        Increased intuition

        Success in business and health

Four nines–Attainment

        Pleasant surprise

        The top


## TENS

Three tens–A blessed business

        Enhancement

        Extensive  travel

        Successful changes

Four tens–A long trip

        Success and fulfillment

        Wealth

## JACKS

Three jacks–Quarrels

                False friends

Four jacks–Parties ( a large gathering)

Multiple jacks in an older woman's reading are an indication of desire for younger men

The person could be involved in a  very serious situation


## QUEENS

Three queens–A clique, gossip, visits

                A private meeting for women

Four queens–Scandals;


## KINGS

Three kings–Publicity

        Promotion

        Progress

        An important consultation

Four kings–Recognition and honor

# COMBINATIONS

There are certain combinations that can change the tone of a reading or add additional dept. A small selection is listed here.

## Ace

A♦ and 10♥ –Wedding or at least a major romance that can lead to marriage

A♦ and 10♣ –A large sum of money

A♦ and A♣ –A change of places/relocation

A♦ and 8♣ –A business proposition

## Twos

2♠ and10♠ –A con game

2♠ and 8♣ –Possibility of jail

2♠ and 5♦ –A surprise party

## Sevens

7♦ and Q♦ –Serious quarrels

7♦ and Q♣ –Uncertainty

7♦ and Q♥ –Good news

7♦ and Q♦ –Wealth

7♠ and 8♠ –A false friend

7♠ and A face card–False friend

## Eights

8♠ and 5♠ –A jealous rival

8♦ and 7♦ –Gossip; A lotto win (when one is next to the other)

8♠ and 9♠ –A health problem

## Nines

9♦ and 8♥ –Journey; Considerable undertakings

9♦ and 8♠ –Sickness

9♦ and 8♣ –A deep lasting love

9♦ and 10♦ –News; A journey over seas

9♥ and 3♦ –A stable love affair

9♥ and K♥ –Lucky for lovers

9♠ and 7♦ –A loss of money or business loss

♦

♣

♥

♠

## Tens

10♦ and 7♠ –Delay

10♦ and 8♣ –Journey

10♣ and A♦ –Large sum of money

10♣ and any Ace and a King–An offer of marriage

# PREPARING TO READ

A serious student of cartomancy would certainly wish to respect the power and potential of the cards. This is done by taking care to treat the cards as if they are a real entity. The first step is to select a pack (or deck) that appeals to you, where the design is pleasing to see. This refers to the back of the card design only. The face (front) of the cards should be the traditional format of a bridge size pack of cards, that is the traditional court/picture cards with the double image, and regular size pips with traditional suit symbols ( no large or jumbo pips and no designs or pictures on the cards).

Once the pack has been selected, it becomes a personal pack and proper care is necessary. The pack used for your readings should not be handled by others or used for playing games. The pack will take on your energy and should be stored properly when not in use. When the cards are not in use place them in a fabric made from a natural fiber (silk or cotton) of a color that appeals to you. This can be a bag to store and carry the cards or it can be a wrapper for the cards in order to store them in another container such as a small wooden box.

Before trying your skills on others memorize a word or short phrase for each card in the pack which sums up the meaning of the card. Try to see each layout as a story. This takes practice, practice, practice.

When you are ready to read for yourself or some one else, create a ritual to help you set a proper mood and prepare the space for reading. It is extremely important to relax and to focus on the task at hand. Your ritual can include a prayer or invocation, some incense, a candle and a glass of water on the table to clear out any unwanted energy, provide protection and to enhance the mood. Sit comfortably with your feet on the floor (legs uncrossed, please) facing south (the direction). Your back should be to the north and the querier should sit directly across from you. Keep your reading area as quiet as possible, background music and people talking can be distracting.

Use your own cards for reading, using someone else's pack can result in a superficial reading especially if the pack has been opened and handled or used by others. When you are ready, remove the Joker, shuffle the cards until you feel that the mix is sufficient then cut the pack with your left hand into three parts from right to left. Reform the pack into one pile with the left hand, stacking the piles from right to left. The cards are ready to be dealt. You may use your own layout or one of the suggested layouts shown in this book.

# T H E   R E A D I N G

There are some general guidelines and definitions of the cards set out by a few famous cartomancers, but your intuition, your connection with the cards and your experience combine to make the actual reading pertinent. No two people will interpret the cards the same way and as one becomes more familiar with the cards various images will come in addition to the meaning/definitions that have come from other sources.

In any layout, each card represents a different aspect of the particular suit to which it belongs. There are numerical, practical and psychic significance which when combined enhance the message. During the actual reading, study the layout for a few seconds, look at the cards individually and together. Determine which suit dominates. Are there more high cards than low cards? Several high cards in a reading strengthen the influence of each card. Beside the general meaning of the card one must consider the position of the card in the layout and whether the meaning is modified or contradicted by the surrounding cards. Look for pairs and multiples of the cards as these will impact the reading as well. It is very important to listen to the client as part of the reading. When these aspects become a part of the reading, the reader can be sincere and have flexibility to go into depth based on knowledge of the cards, the symbolism and the influences of the position of each card. Keeping these elements in mind, the reading is not controlled by the motives of the client where the reader attempts to tell the client what s/he wants to hear. Instead, the reader becomes a channel for spiritual guidance.

What ever the message from the cards it is important to remember that the cards do not make anything happen. The cards do not predict the future. The cards report what already exists as  possibilities unless some action is taken  to change these possibilities. One of the primary reasons for getting a reading is to determine  how we are doing in our lives at the moment and if we need to take corrective measures.   However, divination is not without order, neither is it chance.  Divination is the universe reflecting what is going on in ourselves and our environment.

# T H E L A Y O U T

The foundation of the reading is the layout or the position in which the cards are revealed. The kind of information or advice desired determines the procedure in which the reader will reveal the cards. There are numerous positions or patterns for placing the cards in order to extract specific information. These positions are called layouts. There are some layouts that have been used for many years and a reader can be quite certain about the general advice/information that can be gleaned from a particular spread and what a position in the spread will mean to the card that falls in that position.

Although many layouts have become standards because of the many years of use and general acceptance it not necessary to use one of these layouts, you can create your own. The function of the layout is to arrange the cards in a manner which allows one to access the messages of the cards.

I have included three of my favorite layouts for you to begin your practice:
A general ten card layout when no specific information is requested.
A quick yes or no layout for when an answer is required for a specific question yet an entire reading is not desirable.
A small spread using four cards to give a quick look at what's in store for a particular day.
In each instance, no matter what the layout, one begins by mixing/shuffling the pack of cards well. There are as many formulas for doing this as there are cartomancers. However, one of the most universal is to mix or shuffle until you, the reader, feel that the pack is prepared. Place the pack on the table in front of you and using the left hand cut the pack from right to left making two additional stacks (three stacks total) then still using the left hand, reform the pack from right to left. Pick up the pack and begin to deal the cards into the layout which you have chosen to use.

## SUGGESTED LAYOUTS

There are numerous layouts for readings, you will eventually create your own.
However, here are a few universal or general ones.

## DAILY SPREAD

Used to access quick information on a short term basis. If you want to find out what to expect for today or on a specific event this is a good layout. Proceed by shuffling the cards until you feel that they are ready or prepared for the reading; using the left hand cut the cards once and replace into a single pack; deal the first four cards from the top of the pack placing them on a surface in the pattern illustrated below:

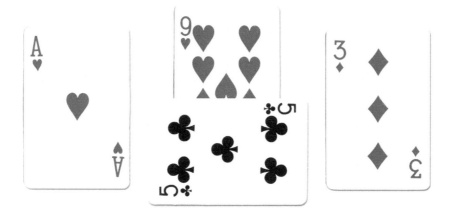

The first card (center card) indicates where you are at the moment or what is most important
Card 2 (across the center card) is the biggest influence
Card 3 (left of center) represents the foundation
Card 4 (right of center) represents suggested actions and options

## YES OR NO QUESTION

Shuffle as indicated above; then using the left hand, cut the cards from right to left making two additional stacks for a total of three stacks. Take the bottom card from each stack and place it on a flat surface in front of you.

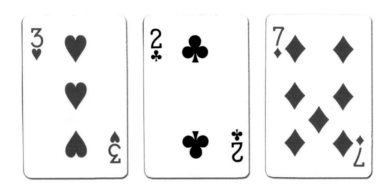

Three (3) black cards mean NO. (The answer to your question is no)

Two (2) black cards and one (1) red card–a "soft" no (maybe)

Three (3) red cards mean YES

Two (2) red cards and one (1) black card mean "yes" but with some reservations.

## GENERAL READING

This type of reading is good for when a person has no particular concern or when time is a factor (I used this one for years on the Psychic hot lines, at fairs and festivals). Shuffle as described and cut with the left hand making three (total) stacks and reforming into one stack before dealing. Use the following format:

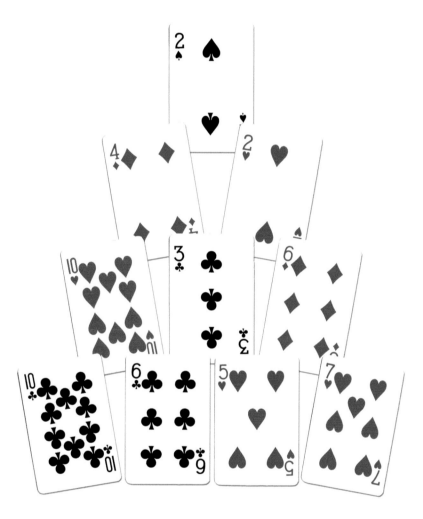

Line 1 (top card) gives the overall influence based on what is around you at the present.

Line 2 (cards 2 and 3) gives a choice; shows actions to consider.

Line 3 (cards 4, 5 and 6) points out the underlying forces at work in your life.

Line 4 (cards 7, 8, 9 and 10) suggests a course of action in order to alter the outcome if needed;

Card 10 denotes the (probable) outcome.

# READING GUIDELINES

Many people ask questions about cartomancy (playing cards) and tarot readings, if you are getting a reading the following guidelines maybe helpful, wherever you get a reading.

Card readers, palm readers, astrologers etc. are not fortune tellers in the literal sense of the word (your past, present, future and the initials of that special person who will sweep you off your feet). They are primarily intuitive people who understand how to interpret the meanings of the cards or charts. The information brought out in a reading is to help you make choices.

An ethical reader will never tell you that something terrible is going to happen to you. If a reader any where volunteers frightening or mysterious information that you did not ask them about it is a signal to you to be careful. This may be a "hook and line" to lure you in for future readings and more money.

Be suspicious of readers who ask you for personal information, a name and phone number to confirm an appointment is fine, your address or where you work is not information that is needed to get an accurate reading.

Payment should not be rendered until the reading is complete. Pay only for the reader's time, not how many times the cards are laid out. The price should be agreed upon before the reading begins. When the reading is over you should not feel as if you need to return at a later time (for another reading) to get more information on the initial reading.

Should the reader ask for extra money in order to give you more information or gets a strange "block" while reading and cannot continue with out more money...ask why!!! If you are not satisfied with the answer, do not continue. If the reader offers to pray for you, sell you a high priced crystal, prayer cloth or other tokens for help or protection, please, feel free to refuse the offer.

A reader may or may not be psychic. Many readers are not psychic. Everyone has some intuitive or clairvoyant sense. A professional reader is one who has learned to work diligently with her own natural intuitive abilities. Usually an exceptional clairvoyant is modest , rarely advertises her talent  and will not brag about her talent. Don't let anyone charge you extra for a psychic reading, it is easier to read with psychic abilities not harder.

The real purpose of a reading is to answer your questions and to point out options, obstacles and the direction or course your life may take under a given set of circumstances. An ethical reader cannot always give you the answers you want to hear, nor can an absolute answer be given to every question. Even the most intuitive reader will not always be on target. It just does not work that way. The cards sometimes fall in very specific patterns and questions can be answered easily. At other times obstacles and/or options will be pointed out that you should be aware of in certain situations in order to get the results you want. NOTHING IS WRITTEN IN STONE! You can change your own fate if you wish to, but that means changing something about yourself (your attitude, your way of thinking etc.) Which may be the most difficult part of the reading to accept.

Every reader has a different style and many readers agree that in order to get an in depth reading you should interact verbally during the reading. If you open up and focus on your questions it will assist the reader in tuning in to you.

Your reading should be fun and informative. ENJOY!

Printed in the United States
By Bookmasters